TABLE OF CONTENTS

Unless otherwise indicated, all Scripture quotations are taken from the King James Version of the Bible.

The Greatest Day of My Life, Seeds of Wisdom on The Holy Spirit, Volume 14
ISBN 1-56394-108-2/B-116
Copyright © 2001 by **MIKE MURDOCK**
All publishing rights belong exclusively to Wisdom International
Publisher/Editor: Deborah Murdock Johnson
Published by The Wisdom Center · 4051 Denton Hwy. · Ft. Worth, Texas 76117
1-817-759-BOOK · 1-817-759-0300
You Will Love Our Website...! WisdomOnline.com

Printed in the United States of America. All rights reserved under International Copyright Law. Contents and/or cover may not be reproduced in whole or in part in any form without the express written consent of the publisher.

Accuracy Department: To our Friends and Partners...We welcome any comments on errors or misprints you find in our book...Email our department: AccuracyDept@thewisdomcenter.tv. Your aid in helping us excel is highly valued.

The Holy Spirit Is
The Only Person
Capable of Being Satisfied
With You.

-MIKE MURDOCK

Copyright © 2001 by Mike Murdock • Wisdom International
The Wisdom Center • 4051 Denton Hwy. • Ft. Worth. TX 76117

MY PERSONAL TESTIMONY

My life changed dramatically on July 13, 1994.
It happened on a Wednesday morning. I had gone to bed at 5:00 a.m. after working all night long on a very special project. Two hours later, at 7:00 a.m., I was awakened suddenly and completely. An unexplainable, undeniable and awesome Presence was in my room.

Something more powerful than anything I had ever experienced...like an invisible emotional current was pulling me from my bedroom toward my "Secret Place." (This is my private prayer room in a small complex next to my house.) Now, I did not really call it "The Secret Place" at that time. It was simply my Prayer Room. But, that day was to change my understanding of God forever.

Because of the overwhelming and compelling urge to enter into intercession and go to The Secret Place, I thought that perhaps my father had suddenly passed on to be with the Lord. You see, my father, who is over 90 years old, is the greatest intercessor I have known in my lifetime. When I think of my dad, I think of him on his knees, with his hands raised, eyes closed and praying "in the Spirit." It was normal for him to spend six to ten hours a day in his personal and private prayer room. Throughout my entire life, I have never heard my father curse, lie or say a single word that could not be placed on the front of any newspaper in the world. That has always impressed me. He walks with God. Well, I had asked the Lord for many years to put his Mantle of Prayer over my life.

When this incredible, unexplainable and compelling surging current began to *draw me toward*

The Secret Place, I thought the Mantle was being transferred that morning. But, I couldn't feel any real sorrow had he really passed away. There was incredible calm and peace.

So, my second thought was, "Someone must be praying for me." You see, my entire ministry is held up daily by hundreds of people who call my name to God. I need their prayers, their intercession and their spiritual support more than any finances or even words of encouragement. I have built my entire ministry on Matthew 18:18-19, and the Prayer of Agreement. Somehow, from my childhood I received unshakable faith that when two people would pray for something *in the will of God,* every demon in hell had to submit to this penetrating power. God answers prayer. Quite simply.

When I travel, I often ask the audiences to remember "Mike Murdock in prayer every day. In fact, every time you walk into a grocery store and see a little bag of M & M's—let that be a reminder to call the name of Mike Murdock in prayer." Everyone always laughs aloud, but they get the point. And, many have told me over the years that every time they see a little bag of M & M candy, they immediately remember to call my name in prayer. So, I thought that somebody had just interceded and had a breakthrough in prayer for my life because of the overwhelming atmosphere and Presence in my room.

My third thought was more dramatic:
Could this be the burning bush experience I had wanted from the Lord my entire lifetime? I've always admired ministers who experience visitations from angels. Wow! I have begged God in my early years to "please let me *see* an angel, *talk* to an angel." That seemed to be something so remarkable and life

changing. I will never forget having supper with the late Roland Buck who had remarkable encounters with angels. But, these kinds of visitations never happened to me.

Yet, I have always believed that God can give you dramatic encounters that create an unshakable, unmovable confidence in His Assignment for your life— *something that no man can ever make you doubt.* He did it for the Apostle Paul, when his name was Saul, on the Damascus road. He did it for Peter when He sent an angel in to the prison while the church prayed for him. He did it for Moses. The burning bush episode was never doubted, even when people were complaining around him many years later.

God is a *dramatic* God.

God is an *emotional* God.

God creates *unforgettable encounters.*

Normally, upon awakening, I would punch "play" on the tape recorder beside my bed or in my bathroom. I always listen to Scriptures being read while I dress. (Nothing on earth is as important as The Word of God being spoken into your mind, heart and life...every single day. *Nothing.*)

But, this surging, invisible and compelling current was overpowering me. Literally, I felt that time was of such essence—I didn't take time to even turn on the Scripture tape.

I grabbed my clothes. Pulling them on, I took my Bible and rushed out the door. I bounded down the concrete steps beside my swimming pool and crossed the driveway over to the little "guest house complex" next door. (I had turned it into private offices for myself, away from the ministry offices.)

It was the most dramatic day of my lifetime.

I fell in love with The Holy Spirit...as a Person. Not

an experience. Not feeling His power surge through me. Rather, beholding His countenance, His glory, and finding Him to be the Best Friend I would ever have in my life.

Now, I am not merely a religious man with religious experiences. Neither am I a novice in the things of God.

My father and mother were married 63 years. She recently went to be with the Lord. My dad has been a pastor and minister for 62 years or so. I am the third child of a proven, established and precious man of God. Seven children are in our family today. My father is an intercessor. I was raised in a non-stop, continuous atmosphere of praise, worship and continuous prayer life. In my own mind, I remember seeing my father more on his knees than I ever saw him off his knees.

He always had a private room for prayer. Though some of us children had to pile up in one bedroom, Daddy always had his separate room for prayer. (It never occurred to me to question it. That was an accepted habit in our household. Daddy was always in his Prayer Room.)

Now, I also had a powerful and unforgettable encounter with The Holy Spirit at the age of ten. Many call it "the baptism of The Holy Spirit." It was at the altar in Franklin, Louisiana, that I was encouraged by a lady evangelist and her husband, Paul and Alice Cormier, to pursue "the baptism." This was basically considered to be an overwhelming encounter with The Holy Spirit that was accompanied by "an unknown prayer language."

I will never forget it. It was real, wonderful and genuine. Great joy entered my heart. And I was so thrilled that I could tell everyone at the church, at last, I had "experienced the baptism." Then, several years later, about the age of 15 or 16, I experienced another mighty and unforgettable baptism in The Holy Spirit in Beaumont, Texas. This happened on the platform when a wonderful man of God, Harry Hodge, prayed over my life on the platform at the church called Sabine Tabernacle.

But, *none of these experiences can compare with July 13, 1994.*

As I review my entire spiritual journey, I perceive that the body of Christ has an obsession with new spiritual experiences, encouragers and memorable events. There is nothing unholy or unspiritual about this. Most great champions of faith can trace the turning points of their life to a night with God, like Jacob had at Bethel.

Whether you experience unusual laughter, falling under the power of God called "slain in the Spirit" or simply running around a church building in response to the flow of joy...*every experience that brings you closer to God should be celebrated.* Every one of them.

Remember, too, that satan creates memorable experiences. He is an imitator of God, not a Creator. So, everything God does, satan tries to duplicate. I am thankful for every remarkable encounter that has swept me *towards* God's presence.

However, experiences are *never* enough.

Your experience should bring you *to Him.* If your spiritual encounter does not bond you with The Holy Spirit, it has merely been an experience.

1.   The Holy Spirit Is The One Who Changes You. Any experience with Him will create a noticeable difference in your conduct, behavior and even the words that flow from your mouth.

Sometimes, it seems that the church sees The Holy Spirit as the wonderful proprietor of a grocery store of blessings. Just like grocery stores sell candy, fruit and many wonderful "gifts," too many are coming away from His power and experiences discussing the "toys and candy."

The Holy Spirit does not want His gifts and manifestations to mesmerize you, paralyze you and become your focus.

2.   He Expects You To Listen To Him Continuously.

3.   He Expects You To Glorify Jesus In Your Life.

Most of us are like the inexperienced country kid visiting a city market for the first time. We are trancelike in our response and never stay around the store long enough to know the proprietor...who makes it all happen.

I would trade every discovery of my lifetime (including my knowledge of the alphabet) for what I discovered about The Holy Spirit on July 13, 1994.

My life changed in many ways.

My attitude changed forever.

The searching ended.

That invisible quest for "answers" stopped. I knew I had just found "The Answer" to every important question of life. The unrest stopped. The discontentment was over.

I lost all fear of man and what men could do to me. Every ounce of fear regarding any potential failure dissolved into nothing. I lost completely, the fear of criticism. The need for encouragement and affirmation from others evaporated. (It simply ceased to add anything to me for someone to compliment me in any way.) It didn't matter any more. His opinion alone mattered.

He was enough.

His presence, pleasing and pleasuring Him and the look on His countenance has become my *obsession*. Two statements soon came from my lips that had never been uttered before in my whole lifetime. But, I was able to make after July 13, 1994:

First, when one of my best friends called and asked me how things were going, I had to honestly make this statement to him. Never, in 50 years of living, had I ever made such a statement. *"I don't know how Heaven could possibly be better than this earth."* That almost sounds blasphemous. How could anyone say such a thing with all the problems on earth? Simple—I could not feel any pain whatsoever, emotionally, mentally, financially or spiritually, of anything going on in my life. Things were in bad shape in some areas—but I could not *feel any of the pain or discomfort from it.* Today, I know why this happened. You see, everybody shouts and gets excited over Heaven. It is quite acceptable to believe that it's not streets of gold in Heaven that makes everyone happy. It is the presence of God. The Holy Spirit, Jesus, the Father—it is *their presence* that makes Heaven a Heaven.

Well, if this is really true—*then His presence on earth could keep us just as happy now*...before we ever leave here...if we are focused *totally* on Him.

Now, there have been days and some weeks since then that my focus has been *broken*. Earth contains warfare. Heaven does not. So, our inner battle here is to maintain total focus on Him *continuously*. In Heaven, no distractions exist.

Second, I was able to make a statement to him that was a first again—*"I cannot think of anything that could possibly improve my life."* Can you imagine such arrogance or pride or bliss? But it was true. This was incredibly unusual for me. I am in constant pursuit of excellence. There has never been a day in my life that I could not think of many things to improve my life! Hundreds! But, after developing an obsession with The Holy Spirit and His presence, it has occurred and been very true. *Nothing else on earth is really necessary for your total joy* (Psalm 16:11).

I looked into the face of a pastor friend some months ago. He asked, "What are your goals and dreams for your ministry? Where do you see your ministry going in the coming years? What is your vision and dream?"

I thought for a good while before answering him. I knew my answer might be misunderstood or misinterpreted. I wasn't trying to be cocky and arrogant. I knew that my answer would make me sound very prideful. But, I went ahead and told him my heart.

"*I am already there.* There is nothing else I'm obsessed in trying to do or achieve. I am *already* where I have been wanting to go."

He looked stunned.

"Are you telling me that you have *arrived?*" He looked incredulous and shocked. Actually, disbelieving.

Well, I knew that this did not show my humble side at all. But, I had to be honest with him.

"Yes," I replied slowly. "Yes, I suppose I *have* arrived."

"I've never heard anybody in my entire life say that they had arrived!"

"Well, don't get mad at everybody for it. Everyone ought to know if they have arrived at where they've been going!" I laughed.

Then I continued, "Let me explain. I wrote a song like this, 'You are where I have been going! Holy Spirit, You've been my destination all this time.'"

Everything inside you is moving toward something.

The *success* teachers tell us it is a dream to be birthed. *Relationship* teachers tell us that it is a "soul mate." *Religious* leaders teach that you are in search of "the meaning of life." Philosophers focus on "your *destiny*." *Your quest is for The Holy Spirit.* He created you. He formed you. He skillfully sculptured your life. You are *empty* unless He enters your life. You are *blind* unless He opens your eyes. You are *deaf* to the incredible sounds on earth unless He unlocks your ears. You are *lost* unless He reveals the way.

The Holy Spirit is the mystery for which everyone is searching. He is the Person Jesus told us to wait for, *look* for...that would continue His presence on the earth, after His ascension.

Now, some of the occurrences on that Wednesday morning, July 13, are "unlawful for me to utter." The Holy Spirit will not permit me to discuss them in detail. Perhaps it is my private "burning bush" encounter. Some of the details must be withheld. Sometimes, The Holy Spirit gives us special secrets between us and Him—that's what makes the relationship so different and unique with Him.

However, there is not a single doubt in me that I have found the *Greatest Secret of the Universe*—the constant presence of The Holy Spirit will satisfy you beyond your imagination. He is who you are looking for. I know it *without a doubt.*

I call Him, "the One who stayed."

Now, I'm not a theologian. I understand little about the mystery of the Godhead. Those who claim great knowledge about the Godhead seem to be joyless. I refuse to be mentored by The Unhappy. I *do* believe...Jesus is making intercession in Heaven for us today and He assigned One who would never leave us nor forsake us, The Holy Spirit.

God's Only Pain Is
To Be Doubted;
His Only Pleasure Is
To Be Believed.

-MIKE MURDOCK

Copyright © 2001 by Mike Murdock • Wisdom International
The Wisdom Center • 4051 Denton Hwy. • Ft. Worth, TX 76117

≈ 1 ≈

THE HOLY SPIRIT IS A PERSON

He Is Not Wind, Fire or A White Dove.
Jesus knew this. He taught us, "And I will pray the Father, and He shall give you another Comforter, that He may abide with you for ever," (John 14:16).
He is not an "it."
He is..."Him."
You see, the pictures, metaphors and emblems used in the Bible can easily be misunderstood.
He Is A Person, Not Merely A Presence. He is a Person who has a presence, an atmosphere emanating from Him. I think the word "Spirit" confuses many.
"Oh, she has such a wonderful *spirit* about her!" said a minister's wife to me. She was referring to the *attitude* of another lady.
"Oh, I love the *spirit* in this church!" This kind of statement refers to the atmosphere and climate existing in a building.
The Holy Spirit Is Not An Attitude, Atmosphere or Environment. He is a Person who talks, thinks, plans and is incredibly articulate. He is The *Voice* of the Godhead to us. Read John 16:13, "...He shall not speak of Himself; but whatsoever He shall hear, that shall He speak." A presence or an atmosphere does not talk! A *person* speaks.
A presence or an atmosphere does not have a will,

a mind or a *plan*. Thoughts have presence. Animals generate a presence. But *The Holy Spirit is much more than a presence.* You see, aroma is not really the food. The stink is not the skunk! The bark is not the dog. The quack is not the duck.

His presence is *evidence* of His Person.

Few people know this. That is why they never discuss their problems with Him. Most believe that He is a silent wind influencing people.

Jesus Recognized Him As A Mentor. "He shall teach you all things," (John 14:26).

He is not merely fog or wind.

He is not merely fire or rain.

He is not merely a white dove at a baptismal service. If He were wind, He could not mentor men. If He were a white bird, He could not teach you. (See John 14:26.) If He were merely fire, He could not impart counsel. The Holy Spirit simply uses various pictures of Himself to reveal His working, His nature and various qualities.

The Holy Spirit Can Enter Your Life Like Water— Refreshing You. "For I will pour water upon him that is thirsty, and floods upon the dry ground: I will pour My Spirit upon thy Seed, and My blessing upon thine offspring: And they shall spring up as among the grass, as willows by the water courses," (Isaiah 44:3-4). But, He is a *Person.*

The Holy Spirit Can Enter Your Life Like Fire— Purifying You. "And there appeared unto them cloven tongues like as of fire, and it sat upon each of them. And they were all filled with the Holy Ghost, and began to speak with other tongues, as the Spirit gave them utterance," (Acts 2:3-4). But, He is a *Person.*

The Holy Spirit Can Move Suddenly And Quickly In Your Life—Like Wind. "And suddenly there came a sound from Heaven as of a rushing mighty wind, and it filled all the house," (Acts 2:2). But, He is a Person.

The Holy Spirit Will Come To You The Way That You Need Him The Most. He can come as a gentle *Nurturer*—like a mother nurturing her starving and dependent child. He can come as a brilliant and articulate *Advisor*—when you are facing a difficult decision. He can come as a comforting *Healer*—when you have been scarred and tormented from a battle.

The Holy Spirit Is A Person. When you embrace this, your Christian experience will change dramatically and satisfy every part of your heart and life.

The Holy Spirit Created You

You Are His Greatest Product.

Job knew this. "The Spirit of God hath made me, and the breath of the Almighty hath given me life," (Job 33:4).

Your Personality, Body And Everything About You Is The Design of The Holy Spirit. Think of this incredible body that functions miraculously. "I will praise Thee; for I am fearfully and wonderfully made: marvellous are Thy works; and that my soul knoweth right well," (Psalm 139:14).

Your Body Is Even The Temple of The Holy Spirit. "What? know ye not that your body is the temple of the Holy Ghost which is in you, which ye have of God, and ye are not your own?" (1 Corinthians 6:19).

Remember: *The Holy Spirit Is A Person.*

Our Prayer Together...
"Holy Spirit, teach me to walk and learn from You, my Mentor, my Companion, The Holy Spirit. You are not fire, wind or rain. You are the Holy One Who created me. In Jesus' name. Amen."

The Word of God Is
The Wisdom of God.

-MIKE MURDOCK

Copyright © 2001 by Mike Murdock • Wisdom International
The Wisdom Center • 4051 Denton Hwy. • Ft. Worth, TX 76117

～ 2 ～

THE HOLY SPIRIT IS THE AUTHOR OF THE WORD OF GOD

Your Bible Is His Gift To You.

The Holy Spirit Breathed Through Men, The Holy Scriptures. "For the prophecy came not in old time by the will of man: but holy men of God spake as they were moved by the Holy Ghost," (2 Peter 1:21).

When You Quote The Bible, You Are Quoting The Holy Spirit. He is articulate, brilliant and authored the words of God to us today. (See 2 Peter 1:21.)

The Holy Spirit Inspired Holy Men of God To Write The Bible To Correct Those In Error. "All scripture is given by inspiration of God, and is profitable for doctrine, for reproof, for correction, for instruction in righteousness: That the man of God may be perfect," (2 Timothy 3:16-17). Oh, think of this glorious Bible we carry around every day! The Holy Spirit spoke every word through 40 people sensitive to Him, over a 1600 year period of time.

▶ He wanted to breathe His *life* into you.

▶ He wanted His *energy* imparted to you.

▶ He wanted His *Wisdom* deposited in you.

The Holy Spirit Gave You The Word of God As Your

Special Weapon, The Sword of The Spirit. "And take the helmet of salvation, and the sword of the Spirit, which is the Word of God," (Ephesians 6:17). It is the weapon of The Holy Spirit—the weapon He uses against satan. His *Words* are His destructive weapons that destroy the things of satan.

Jesus Used The Weapon of The Word, The Sword of The Spirit. When satan tempted Him, Jesus simply answered with the words of The Holy Spirit! "It is written, That man shall not live by bread alone, but by every word of God," (Luke 4:4). So, satan reacts instantly to any words of The Holy Spirit that you believe, embrace and stand on in total faith. (See Luke 4.)

So, The Holy Spirit Always Anticipates Your Warfare. He understands battle. It matters to Him. Your winning is on His mind all the time. He truly has not left you comfortless. He has put His weapon in your *hand,* in your *mouth,* in your *life...*The Word of God.

Memorize His Word. The Word of God is the only weapon satan cannot withstand.

Your Bible contains 66 books. These 66 books contain 1189 chapters. Someone estimated that the entire Bible can be read within 56 hours.

5 Helpful Hints For Reading Your Bible

The Word of God Is The Instrument The Holy Spirit Uses To Change You.

▶ You *experience* The Holy Spirit through *visitation*...of His presence.

▶ You *know* The Holy Spirit through *meditation* on His Word.

1. **Establish A Daily Habit.**

2. **Read It At The Same Place Every Day!**
3. **Read It At The Same Time Each Day.**
4. **Become An Expert On One Topic In The Bible.**
5. **Talk Scriptures In Every Conversation.**

Remember: *The Holy Spirit Is The Author of The Word of God.*

RECOMMENDED INVESTMENTS:
The Greatest Success Habit on Earth (Book/B-80/32 pages/$3)
The Holy Spirit Handbook, Vol. 1 (Book/B-100/153 pages/$15)
The Book That Changed My Life (Book/B-117/32 pages/$7)
The School of The Holy Spirit (Series 1) The Greatest Secret of
   The Universe (6 tapes/TS-50/$30)

Crisis Is Simply
An Invitation
To A Miracle.

-MIKE MURDOCK

Copyright © 2001 by Mike Murdock • Wisdom International
The Wisdom Center • 4051 Denton Hwy. • Ft. Worth, TX 76117

❧ 3 ❧

THE HOLY SPIRIT DECIDES THE TIMING OF EACH MAJOR TESTING IN YOUR LIFE

You Will Be Tested.

The Holy Spirit Guides You Into Your Wilderness of Battle. He did it in the life of Jesus and will in your life as well. "And Jesus...was led by the Spirit into the wilderness, Being forty days tempted of the devil," (Luke 4:1-2).

The Holy Spirit Will Test You Prior To Your Promotion. The purpose of your testing is not mere survival. It is to *qualify* you for promotion. The entire earth is motivated by *reward.* God planned it. It is unnatural to pursue decrease. It is normal to pursue increase.

The Holy Spirit led Jesus into the wilderness. He brought Him into a place of aloneness. *Aloneness Always Concludes With A Battle.*

The battle for your *focus.*

The battle for your *mind.*

The Place of Testing Is Always The *Place of Trust.* So, The Holy Spirit will always carefully time your season of testing...to qualify you for a season of reward.

He does not merely give you a reward for surviving your test. He provides you a test *to qualify you for the rewards*. He desires you to *give*.

God Keeps Using Everything He Has Made. He used the *stars* to motivate Abraham's faith for children. He used *water* to turn a marriage into a place of miracles when the wedding party ran out of wine. He used *clay and spittle* to unlock the faith of a blind man. He used a *fish* to give Peter money.

He Uses Satan To Qualify You For A Blessing.

Everything in your life is a reward or a test. The Holy Spirit always brings you to a place of decision. He leads you to a place of testing.

► The Holy Spirit knows your *tempter.*

► The Holy Spirit anticipates your *testing.*

► The Holy Spirit provides the *answer.*

Your Answers Are Always In The Word of God. Always. When Jesus was being tempted, He did not cry out for a special music so that He could *access* the right frame of mind. He never said, "I must get back to the synagogue. I had no business coming out here alone." No, Jesus knew the answers. As He began to quote the eternal Word of God, satan was *immobilized.*

Jesus passed the test. The Anointing continued.

► Your *testing* qualifies you for *promotion.*

► Your *promotion* qualifies you for *rewards.*

► Your *rewards* increase the flow of your *joy.*

The Holy Spirit Never Makes Mistakes. So, relax during testing. He will not fail. He knows your enemy. Your enemy *always* makes mistakes. *Always.*

Your Only Responsibility Is To Trust The Holy Spirit. Keep His words in your mind, your mouth and in every conversation.

His Words Are Your Weapons. "For the weapons of

our warfare are not carnal, but mighty through God to the pulling down of strong holds," (2 Corinthians 10:4).

The Holy Spirit Will Not Permit The Test To Be Too Great. "There hath no temptation taken you but such as is common to man: but God is faithful, Who will not suffer you to be tempted above that ye are able; but will with the temptation also make a way to escape, that ye may be able to bear it," (1 Corinthians 10:13).

You Will Experience A Double Portion of Influence And Provision As You Overcome Your Present Testing. It happened to Job. "And the Lord turned the captivity of Job, when he prayed for his friends: also the Lord gave Job twice as much as he had before," (Job 42:10). That is why it is important for you to be *patient,* knowing that God will answer your prayers. "Behold, we count them happy which endure. Ye have heard of the patience of Job, and have seen the *end* of the Lord; that the Lord is very pitiful, and of tender mercy," (James 5:11).

Remember: *The Holy Spirit Decides The Timing of Each Major Testing In Your Life.*

Our Prayer Together...

"Holy Spirit, thank You for the *season* of testing. You have decided the timing, my victory and will empower me through every season. You have already decided that *my enemy will fail.* I will overcome. You will receive the glory and praise for it. Today, I am patiently praising You for this wonderful season of promotion I am walking toward. In Jesus' name. Amen."

The Atmosphere
You Create
Determines The Product
You Produce.

-MIKE MURDOCK

Copyright © 2001 by Mike Murdock • Wisdom International
The Wisdom Center • 4051 Denton Hwy. • Ft. Worth, TX 76117

∾ 4 ∾

THE HOLY SPIRIT RESPONDS TO WORSHIPFUL SINGING

Singing Is Very Important To The Holy Spirit.
The Holy Spirit sings over you as well. "The Lord thy God in the midst of thee is mighty; He will save, He will rejoice over thee with joy; He will rest in His love, *He will joy over thee with singing,*" (Zephaniah 3:17).

Many people cannot imagine our God singing. But, He does! I can picture this so clearly in my heart. The Holy Spirit is like a mother leaning over the bed of her small child and singing, "Sleep, my precious baby! Sleep, precious love of my life. I will watch over you and protect you, until the day that follows this night."

10 Facts You Should Know About Singing

1. The Holy Spirit Wants You To Sing When You Enter His Presence. "Come before His presence with singing," (Psalm 100:2).

Sounds are wonderful to The Holy Spirit! Listen to the birds today as they sing out in wonderment! Listen to the sounds of animals, the wind blowing through the trees and even the wonderful love sounds of those family members close to you. Singing is an essential part of this world. That is why The Holy Spirit wants you to be aware of His fervent desire to hear you sing to Him.

2. Sing To Him Specifically, Not Just To People. I have written over 5,700 songs throughout my lifetime. Yet, the songs I *love* to sing are the Love Songs to The Holy Spirit. I call them, "Songs from The Secret Place." Hundreds of songs have been birthed in my heart since I *fell in love* with The Holy Spirit on July 13, 1994.

3. Sing From Your Heart, Not Your Mind. He does not need fancy words or beautiful sounds. He simply wants you to open your heart and let the "love sounds" flow from you. (See 1 Corinthians 13.)

4. Sing In Your Prayer Language, Too. The Apostle Paul understood the incredible power of singing. "I will sing with the Spirit, and I will sing with the understanding also," (1 Corinthians 14:15). "Paul and Silas prayed, and sang praises unto God," (Acts 16:25).

5. The Holy Spirit Wants You To Sing Together With Other Saints. "Let the word of Christ dwell in you richly in all Wisdom; teaching and admonishing one another in psalms and hymns and spiritual songs, singing with grace in your hearts to the Lord," (Colossians 3:16).

6. When You Sing To The Holy Spirit, Evil Spirits Will Leave. King Saul discovered this under the anointed music ministry of David. In fact, the music of David refreshed Saul. "And it came to pass, when the evil spirit from God was upon Saul, that David took an harp, and played with his hand: so Saul was refreshed, and was well, and the evil spirit departed from him," (1 Samuel 16:23).

That is why I placed 24 speakers on the trees in my seven-acre yard. I cannot tell you how wonderful it is to walk across my yard, hearing these songs to The Holy Spirit. Also, stereo speakers have been installed throughout the rooms of my home, playing songs to The Holy Spirit continuously. Words cannot describe the effect it has on my heart and mind. *The Holy Spirit Comes When He Is Celebrated.*

Invest in an excellent, quality stereo and make music a major part of every day. It is worth every penny. Your *mind* will respond. Your *heart* will find new fire. Your *body* will receive a surging of new energy and vitality. Most of all, The Holy Spirit will manifest His presence.

7. **Singers Were Often The Reason For Victories Against The Enemies of God.** "And when they began to sing and to praise, the Lord set ambushments against the children of Ammon, Moab, and mount Seir, which were come against Judah; and they were smitten," (2 Chronicles 20:22).

► Your singing to The Holy Spirit *will create an atmosphere of thanksgiving.*
► Your singing will greatly *influence your focus.*
► Your singing can dispel *every demonic influence designed to distract you.*
► Your singing will arouse the energy and passion of your own body to focus on your Creator.
► Your singing is an act of obedience to The Holy Spirit. (See Psalm 100:2.)

8. **Your Singing Can Affect Nature Itself.** Read again the incredible story of Paul and Silas in prison. Everything was going against them. But, they understood the *Weapon of Singing.* "And at midnight Paul and Silas prayed, and sang praises unto God:... And suddenly there was a great earthquake, so that the

foundations of the prison were shaken: and immediately all the doors were opened," (Acts 16:25-26).

9. Singing Can Make Your Enemy Demoralized, Discouraged And Decide To Move Away From You. Paul watched this happen when he and Silas sang in the prison. "And the keeper of the prison awaking out of his sleep, and seeing the prison doors open, he drew out his sword, and would have killed himself, supposing that the prisoners had been fled," (Acts 16:27).

10. Singing Can Change Everything Around Your Life. Everything. So, begin this very moment. Close this book and begin to sing *aloud* to The Holy Spirit. Your words may be simple, but they will become powerful.

So, you and I can learn from the champions. Those who have conquered in battle have discerned the hidden and mysterious power of singing. You must do it in your own life today! "Saying, I will declare Thy name unto my brethren, in the midst of the church will I sing praise unto Thee," (Hebrews 2:12).

Remember: *The Holy Spirit Responds To Worshipful Singing.*

Our Prayer Together...

"Holy Spirit, thank You for revealing the Weapon of Singing to my life. I will sing...when things go wrong or right. I will sing *regardless of my circumstances.* I will sing for the purpose of *honoring You* and obeying You! I will sing *songs of remembrance,* because I remember every blessing You have given me over the years! I will sing *continuously,* knowing that as I sing, angels come and minister to me! I will sing with *victory,* knowing that demonic spirits are becoming fragmented and confused when they hear my words. I will sing, knowing that my mouth is my *deliverer!* I will teach *my children* to sing to You! I will have songs played in my home, in my car and on my job continuously...to honor Your presence! *Thank You for singing to me* over my life! In Jesus' name. Amen."

RECOMMENDED INVESTMENTS:
The Holy Spirit Handbook, Vol. 1 (Book/B-100/153 pages/$15)
The 3 Most Important Things in Your Life (Book/B-101/
    240 pages/$15)
The Holy Spirit Handbook (6 tapes/TS-29/$30)
Love Songs to The Holy Spirit (6 music tapes/TS-59/$30)

What Happens
In Your Mind
Usually Happens In Time.

-MIKE MURDOCK

Copyright © 2001 by Mike Murdock • Wisdom International
The Wisdom Center • 4051 Denton Hwy. • Ft. Worth, TX 76117

⇜ 5 ⇝

THE HOLY SPIRIT CAN REVEAL FUTURE EVENTS TO YOU BEFORE THEY EVEN HAPPEN

————⇒▷◦◁⇐————

The Holy Spirit Sees Far Ahead.
He will show you events before they ever occur. Jesus promised this would happen. "He will shew you things to come," (John 16:13).

The Holy Spirit Is The Spirit of Prophecy. "For the prophecy came not in old time by the will of man: but holy men of God spake as they were moved by the Holy Ghost," (2 Peter 1:21).

The Holy Spirit Spoke Ahead of Time About Scoffers Making Light of The Coming of Christ In The Last Days. "That ye may be mindful of the words which were spoken before by the holy prophets, and of the commandment of us the apostles of the Lord and Saviour: Knowing this first, that there shall come in the last days scoffers, walking after their own lusts, And saying, Where is the promise of His coming?" (2 Peter 3:2-4).

The Holy Spirit Gave The Great Prophet, Samuel, Photographs of Future Events. "Now the Lord had told Samuel in his ear a day before Saul came, saying, Tomorrow about this time I will send thee a man out of the land of Benjamin, and thou shalt anoint him to be captain over My people Israel, that he may save My people out of the hand of the Philistines," (1 Samuel 9:15-16). *The Holy Spirit Inspires, Anoints And Qualifies Men And Women To Prophesy To Others As Well.* "For to one is given by the Spirit the word of Wisdom; to another the word of knowledge by the same Spirit; To another the working of miracles; to another prophecy; to another discerning of spirits; to another divers kinds of tongues; to another the interpretation of tongues," (1 Corinthians 12:8, 10).

The Holy Spirit Gave Jeremiah Photographs of His Future From The Lord. "Then the word of the Lord came unto me, saying; Before I formed thee in the belly, I knew thee; and before thou camest forth out of the womb I sanctified thee, and I ordained thee a prophet unto the nations," (Jeremiah 1:4-5).

The Holy Spirit Is Not A Respecter of Persons. Throughout the ages He places pictures of the future in the heart of those He loves. He will do it for you.

God Showed Abraham Pictures of His Future Greatness. "And I will make of thee a great nation, and I will bless thee, and make thy name great; and thou shalt be a blessing: And I will bless them that bless thee...and in thee shall all families of the earth be blessed," (Genesis 12:2-3).

You must *receive* a picture of your future.

You must *believe* that photograph.

You must *water* that Seed of Tomorrow.

You must receive it from The Holy Spirit.

You must *protect* that picture.

Nobody else can do it for you. Nobody else will believe it. You must embrace it, receive it and *protect* that picture. That incredible Photograph of Tomorrow is planted within you *by The Holy Spirit* who formed you even in your mother's womb. *The Holy Spirit Gave Joseph A Picture of His Future In A Dream.* "For, behold, we were binding sheaves in the field, and, lo, my sheaf arose, and also stood upright; and, behold, your sheaves stood round about, and made obeisance to my sheaf," (Genesis 37:7). Joseph visualized himself in the position of *authority.* He visualized others honoring him. His mind changed. His conduct and behavior changed to birth that picture.

What Happens In Your Mind Usually Happens In Time. That is why The Holy Spirit is so important in your life. Your behavior cannot change until He births in you a picture of what He is looking at when He sees you.

He *sees* something you do not see.

He is taking you where you have never been.

He is *planting the Seed* of what you are becoming.

He is the Spirit of Prophecy Who brings the future *into* you—not merely you into your future.

Your Future Has To Move Into You Before You Can Move Into Your Future.

Your Picture of Tomorrow Will Impart A Strength To Endure Your Present Difficulties. Trouble becomes easier to handle when you know that it will not last. Jesus had this picture—"Who for the joy that was set before Him endured the cross, despising the shame, and is set down at the right hand of the throne of God," (Hebrews 12:2). *Jesus Had Confidence In His Resurrection That Enabled Him To Endure His Crucifixion.*

Remember: *The Holy Spirit Can Reveal Future Events To You Before They Even Happen.*

 Our Prayer Together...
"Holy Spirit, You have a specific plan for my life. You already know what tomorrow holds. I *trust*

You. So, I ask You to begin to show me *pictures* of Your future plans for me. Show me those Seeds of Tomorrow that I need to grow. Alter my conduct and my behavior so that it agrees with Your plan for my life. In Jesus' name. Amen."

RECOMMENDED INVESTMENTS:
The Assignment: The Trials & The Triumphs, Vol. 3 (Book/B-97/ 160 pages/$12)
The Assignment: The Pain & The Passion, Vol. 4 (Book/B-98/ 144 pages/$12)
The Law of Recognition (Book/B-114/247 pages/$15)
The Strategy of Hourly Obedience (6 tapes/TS-08/$30)
The School of The Holy Spirit (Series 1) The Greatest Secret of The Universe (6 tapes/TS-50/$30)
The Assignment: The Dream & The Destiny (6 tapes/TS-52/$30)

∽ 6 ∽

THE HOLY SPIRIT DECIDES YOUR ASSIGNMENT, THE PROBLEM YOU WERE CREATED TO SOLVE

Your Assignment Has Already Been Decided.
The Holy Spirit Decided Your Assignment. "Before I formed thee in the belly I knew thee; and before thou camest forth out of the womb I sanctified thee, and I ordained thee a prophet unto the nations," (Jeremiah 1:5).

Jeremiah believed this. While he was yet in his mother's womb, God had decided that he would become a great deliverer. His responsibility? To accept it, not alter it.

Everything Created Contains An Invisible Instruction. Look inside a watermelon seed. You cannot see it with your natural eye. But, inside that watermelon seed is a command, an Assignment to produce more watermelons.

Everything Created Is A Solution. Your eyes see. Your ears hear. Your hands reach. Your feet walk. Your mouth speaks. Mechanics solve car problems. Lawyers solve legal problems. Dentists solve teeth problems. Mothers solve emotional problems. Ministers solve spiritual problems.

You Were Created To Solve Some Kind of Problem While You Are On The Earth. The Holy Spirit created you. (Read Job 33:4.) He had a reason. That is why He gave you the specific gifts and talents that you have. "Now there are diversities of gifts, but the same Spirit. And there are differences of administrations, but the same Lord," (1 Corinthians 12:4-5).

You Do Not Decide Your Gifts—You Discover Them. "But all these worketh that one and the selfsame Spirit, dividing to every man severally as He will," (1 Corinthians 12:11).

What You Love Is A Clue To Your Assignment. Think for a moment. What is your greatest passion? What excites you and energizes you every day? If you could speak on any one subject, what would that subject be? You see, whatever you love, you will have a Wisdom toward.

Love Is A Signpost To Your Wisdom. A desire *to learn* will emerge toward whatever you have a love for. It may be animals, babies or automobiles. Pay attention to the passion placed within your heart. It is a clue to your Assignment on earth.

What You Hate Is A Clue To Something You Were Created To Correct or Change. When Moses saw an Egyptian beating up an Israelite, an anger rose within him. Why? He was their Deliverer. You may hate alcohol, drugs or child abuse. That is a clue to something you were created to change and correct.

What Grieves You Is A Clue To Something You Were Created To Heal. Pay attention to your tears. Compassion is powerful. It is also a signpost to your Assignment on earth.

Your Assignment Is Geographical. The Holy Spirit knows exactly the town and city where you should live or minister. "Then the Spirit said unto Philip, Go near, and join thyself to this chariot," (Acts 8:29; see also Acts 13:2).

Spiritual Champions Always Depend On The Holy Spirit For Specific Instructions Regarding Their Assignment. "As they ministered to the Lord, and fasted, the Holy Ghost said, Separate Me Barnabas and Saul for the work whereunto I have called them. And when they had fasted and prayed, and laid their hands on them, they sent them away. So they, being sent forth by the Holy Ghost, departed unto Seleucia; and from thence they sailed to Cyprus," (Acts 13:2-4).

You must find the center of your expertise. Nobody else can find it for you. It may not be produced through your logic, questioning, nor even those special personality profile tests that you receive from particular counselors.

The Holy Spirit Alone Knows Your Assignment. You will only discover it in His presence. (See Psalm 26:4-6.)

Remember: *The Holy Spirit Decides Your Assignment, The Problem You Were Created To Solve.*

Our Prayer Together...

"Holy Spirit, You created me for a reason. You know it and want to reveal it to me. Even now, I listen for Your voice. I will *go* anywhere You want me to go. I will *say* anything You want me to say. I will *stay* any place You want me to remain. *Your desires are my desires.* Remove from my life anything that is not of You. Take the wrong people out of my life. Bring the right people into my life. I accept and embrace totally and completely Your Assignment in my life today. In Jesus' name. Amen."

J^{oy} ~ Is The Proof of His Presence.

-MIKE MURDOCK

Copyright © 2001 by Mike Murdock • Wisdom International
The Wisdom Center • 4051 Denton Hwy. • Ft. Worth, TX 76117

➣ 7 ➣

THE HOLY SPIRIT MAY WITHDRAW HIS MANIFEST PRESENCE WHEN HE HAS BEEN OFFENDED

Never Take His Presence Lightly.

"I will go and return to My place, till they acknowledge their offence, and seek My face: in their affliction they will seek Me early," (Hosea 5:15).

The love of God has been so misunderstood. His mercy has been taken for granted by millions.

"Oh, well! God knows my heart," laughed one lady when her pastor asked her why she had not been to church in several months. She had been taking vacations, spending her time out on the lake on Sundays. Yet, she had become so accustomed to ignoring the inner voice of The Holy Spirit, her conscience had become seared and numb.

It Is A Dangerous Attitude To Think That Access To God Is Permanent And Easy.

His Presence keeps you soft toward Him.

His Presence keeps you hungry and thirsty. When you do not pursue His Presence, the danger of becoming calloused and hardened is very real. A minister once told me, "I never dreamed I could get this far from God." As I looked at him, I was shocked. Here sat a man who had preached with fire in his soul, love pouring through his heart, many years before.

But, he had offended The Holy Spirit over and over again. Now, The Holy Spirit had withdrawn. He had even lost his hunger and his thirst for the Presence of God. Do you feel troubled in your spirit? Thank God for such a troubling! Millions have ignored Him so long that the Fire of Desire has died.

Rejection of The Holy Spirit Can Be Fatal. Jesus said it clearly, "Remember Lot's wife," (Luke 17:32). The angels had appeared personally to escort Lot and his family from danger to safety. But, she took it lightly. Their instructions became unimportant. She rebelled. She became a pillar of salt. That is why Jesus wept over Jerusalem.

Consistent Rejection of The Holy Spirit Eventually Produces Desolation. "...your house is left unto you desolate," (Matthew 23:38).

Conversation Can Grieve The Holy Spirit. "Let no corrupt communication proceed out of your mouth, but that which is good to the use of edifying, that it may minister grace unto the hearers. And grieve not the Holy Spirit of God, whereby ye are sealed unto the day of redemption," (Ephesians 4:29-30).

The Presence of The Holy Spirit Yesterday Does Not Guarantee The Presence of God Tomorrow. Look at what happened to Saul. He had known the Anointing. God had selected him. God had touched his life. The prophet of God anointed him. Yet, "the Spirit of the Lord departed from Saul, and an evil spirit from the Lord troubled him," (1 Samuel 16:14).

He died the death of a fool.

The Psalmist Knew The Terrifying Seasons When The Holy Spirit Seemed Withdrawn From Him. David had been with Saul. He watched evil spirits depart as he played his harp. He saw the touch of God on Saul come...*and leave.* He cried out after his own terrible sin with Bathsheba, "Cast me not away from Thy presence; and take not Thy Holy Spirit from me," (Psalm 51:11). Now, theologians laugh at David's confession and pursuit. Thousands of ministers say David was wrong, that The Holy Spirit could not withdraw from him. But, David had observed King Saul's deterioration. Don't kid yourself.

If you have spent much time on the earth, as a minister of the gospel, you will see many from whom The Holy Spirit has withdrawn. No, He doesn't do it easily or quickly. He is long-suffering. He is patient.

But, *repeated rejection of His drawing has devastating results.*

Most have never read these terrifying words in Hosea 5:15: "I will go and return to My place, till they acknowledge their offense, and seek My face: In their affliction, they will seek Me early."

I raise my voice with Hosea today: "Come, and let us return unto the Lord: for He hath torn, and He will heal us; He hath smitten, and He will bind us up. After two days will He revive us: in the third day He will raise us up, and we shall live in His sight. Then shall we know, if we follow on to know the Lord," (Hosea 6:1-3).

The Song of Solomon contains one of the saddest photographs of love rejected and lost. "I opened to my beloved; but my beloved had withdrawn Himself, and was gone: my soul failed when He spake: I sought Him, but I could not find Him; I called Him, but He gave me no answer," (Song of Solomon 5:6).

A Special Note

Satan Often Lies To Someone About The Withdrawing of The Holy Spirit. He makes them feel that it is useless to pray, futile to reach and hopeless to believe for a change. Satan often tells people that they have sinned "the unpardonable sin" when the opposite is true.

How do you know that you have not truly sinned the unpardonable sin? *If you still have a desire for Him, The Holy Spirit is at work.* The Father is the One Who draws you. If you still have within your heart a sincere desire to know God and an appetite to pursue Him, you have not yet sinned the unpardonable sin. You see, only God can draw you. If He is drawing you, it is not too late. You still have a chance for a miraculous experience with Him.

Remember: *The Holy Spirit May Withdraw His Manifest Presence When He Has Been Offended.*

Our Prayer Together...
"Holy Spirit, I am teachable today. I am reachable today. Cleanse me, purify me and draw me toward You. I do not want to take lightly Your presence and the access I have to You. In my failures, You have sustained me and kept alive within me a desire for righteousness. This craving and desire for perfection has come from You, not myself. I ask You to draw me to You today more than You ever have. Turn my heart toward You. Birth within me a hatred for unrighteousness and a love for holy living. You are my God, and I am Your child. In Jesus' name. Amen."

RECOMMENDED INVESTMENTS:
Wisdom For Winning (Book/B-01/228 pages/$10)
The Assignment: The Dream & The Destiny, Vol. 1 (Book/B-74/ 164 pages/$12)
The Assignment: The Anointing & The Adversity, Vol. 2 (Book/B-75/ 192 pages/$12)
The Leadership Secrets of Jesus (Book/B-91/196 pages/$12)

DECISION

Will You Accept Jesus As Your Personal Savior Today?

The Bible says, "That if thou shalt confess with thy mouth the Lord Jesus, and shalt believe in thine heart that God hath raised Him from the dead, thou shalt be saved," (Romans 10:9).

Pray this prayer from your heart today!

"Dear Jesus, I believe that You died for me and rose again on the third day. I confess I am a sinner...I need Your love and forgiveness...Come into my heart. Forgive my sins. I receive Your eternal life. Confirm Your love by giving me peace, joy and supernatural love for others. Amen."

DR. MIKE MURDOCK

is in tremendous demand as one of the most dynamic speakers in America today.

More than 17,000 audiences in over 100 countries have attended his Schools of Wisdom and conferences. Hundreds of invitations come to him from churches, colleges and business corporations. He is a noted author of over 250 books, including the best sellers, *The Leadership Secrets of Jesus* and *Secrets of the Richest Man Who Ever Lived*. Thousands view his weekly television program, *Wisdom Keys with Mike Murdock*. Many attend his Schools of Wisdom that he hosts in many cities of America.

☐ Yes, Mike! I made a decision to accept Christ as my personal Savior today. Please send me my free gift of your book, *31 Keys to a New Beginning* to help me with my new life in Christ.

NAME _____ BIRTHDAY _____

ADDRESS _____

CITY _____ STATE _____ ZIP _____

PHONE _____ E-MAIL _____

Mail to: **The Wisdom Center** · 4051 Denton Hwy. · Ft. Worth, TX 76117
1-817-759-BOOK · 1-817-759-0300
You Will Love Our Website...! WisdomOnline.com

Clip and Mail

DR. MIKE MURDOCK

1 Has embraced his Assignment to Pursue...Proclaim...and Publish the Wisdom of God to help people achieve their dreams and goals.

2 Preached his first public sermon at the age of 8.

3 Preached his first evangelistic crusade at the age of 15.

4 Began full-time evangelism at the age of 19, which has continued since 1966.

5 Has traveled and spoken to more than 17,000 audiences in over 100 countries, including East and West Africa, the Orient, Europe and South America.

6 Noted author of over 250 books, including best sellers, *Wisdom for Winning, Dream Seeds, The Double Diamond Principle, The Law of Recognition* and *The Holy Spirit Handbook.*

7 Created the popular *Topical Bible* series for Businessmen, Mothers, Fathers, Teenagers; *The One-Minute Pocket Bible* series, and *The Uncommon Life* series.

8 The Creator of The Master 7 Mentorship System, an Achievement Program for Believers.

9 Has composed thousands of songs such as "I Am Blessed," "You Can Make It," "God Rides On Wings of Love" and "Jesus, Just The Mention of Your Name," recorded by many gospel artists.

10 Is the Founder and Senior Pastor of The Wisdom Center, in Fort Worth, Texas...a Church with International Ministry around the world.

11 Host of *Wisdom Keys with Mike Murdock,* a weekly TV Program seen internationally.

12 Has appeared often on TBN, CBN, BET, Daystar, Inspirational Network, LeSea Broadcasting and other television network programs.

13 Has led over 3,000 to accept the call into full-time ministry.

44

THE MINISTRY

1 **Wisdom Books & Literature** - Over 250 best-selling Wisdom Books and 70 Teaching Tape Series.

2 **Church Crusades** - Multitudes are ministered to in crusades and seminars throughout America in "The Uncommon Wisdom Conferences." Known as a man who loves pastors, he has focused on church crusades for over 43 years.

3 **Music Ministry** - Millions have been blessed by the anointed songwriting and singing of Mike Murdock, who has made over 15 music albums and CDs available.

4 **Television** - *Wisdom Keys with Mike Murdock,* a nationally-syndicated weekly television program.

5 **The Wisdom Center** - The Church and Ministry Offices where Dr. Murdock speaks weekly on Wisdom for The Uncommon Life.

6 **Schools of The Holy Spirit** - Mike Murdock hosts Schools of The Holy Spirit in many churches to mentor believers on the Person and Companionship of The Holy Spirit.

7 **Schools of Wisdom** - In many major cities Mike Murdock hosts Schools of Wisdom for those who want personalized and advanced training for achieving "The Uncommon Dream."

8 **Missions Outreach** - Dr. Mike Murdock's overseas outreaches to over 100 countries have included crusades in East and West Africa, the Orient, Europe and South America.

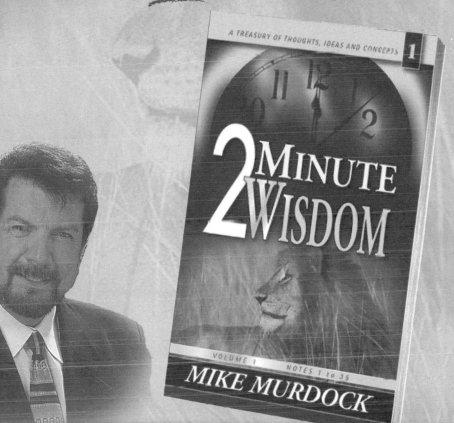

35 Success-Notes...!

That Can Unlock Your Dreams And Goals!

Order Your FREE Personal Copy Today!

A TREASURY OF THOUGHTS, IDEAS AND CONCEPTS 1

2 MINUTE WISDOM

VOLUME 1 · NOTES 1 to 35

MIKE MURDOCK

Download It For Free On WisdomOnline.com

THE WISDOM CENTER
4051 Denton Highway · Fort Worth, TX 76117

1-817-759-BOOK
1-817-759-0300

You Will Love Our Website...!
WisdomOnline.com

A Miracle Is In Your Hands...

Give Two Friends A Subscription To The Wisdom Digest.

Every Issue Of The Wisdom Digest Contains Fascinating Articles And A Special Prayer Request Section, With An Enclosed Postage-Paid Envelope...For Returning To Dr. Murdock And The Prayer Team At The Wisdom Center. Twice A Day Your Prayer Requests Are Presented To The Lord.

Take The Time And Ask For The Miracle Of A FREE Subscription For Yourself And Two Friends Today!

Yes, Mike, I Would Like My Friend(s) To Receive *The Wisdom Digest*.

❏

NAME _____

ADDRESS _____

CITY _____ STATE _____ ZIP _____

PHONE _____ EMAIL _____

❏

NAME _____

ADDRESS _____

CITY _____ STATE _____ ZIP _____

PHONE _____ EMAIL _____

Enclosed is my Special Seed of $_____ for your Ministry. Please send me my own Gift Subscription of The Wisdom Digest to the address below:

Method of payment (your transaction may be electronically deposited.)

❏ MONEY ORDER ❏ CHECK ❏ VISA
❏ MASTER CARD ❏ AMEX ❏ DISCOVER

CARD # _____ - _____ - _____ - _____

EXP. DATE _____ / _____ TOTAL ENCLOSED $ _____

SIGNATURE _____

Your Seed-Faith Offerings are used to support The Wisdom Center, and all of its programs. The Wisdom Center reserves the right to redirect funds as needed in order to carry out our charitable purpose. In the event The Wisdom Center receives more funds for the project than needed, the excess will be used for another worthy outreach. (Your transactions may be electronically deposited.)

❏

NAME _____

ADDRESS _____

CITY _____ STATE _____ ZIP _____

PHONE _____ EMAIL _____

THE WISDOM CENTER

4051 Denton Hwy. • Fort Worth, TX 76117 • 817-759-BOOK • 817-759-0300 • WisdomOnline.com

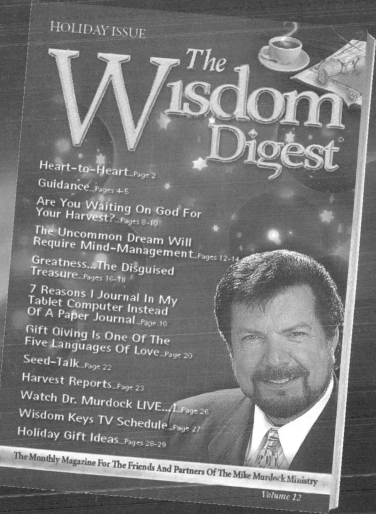

HOLIDAY ISSUE

The Wisdom Digest

The Monthly Magazine For The Friends And Partners Of The Mike Murdock Ministry

Volume 12

Don't Miss An Issue Of The Wisdom Digest With Life-Changing Articles Featuring Topics On The Following:

- ▶ Personal Success/Finances
- ▶ Marriage And Home
- ▶ Foundational Biblical Studies
- ▶ For Singles Only
- ▶ Your Job And Career
- ▶ Overcoming
- ▶ The Spirit Life
- ▶ Your Assignment

Request Your FREE Subscription Today!

THE WISDOM CENTER

4051 Denton Hwy. • Fort Worth, TX 76117 • 817-759-BOOK • 817-759-0300 • WisdomOnline.com

7 Hidden Ingredients In Every Miracle...

The Hidden Secrets That Cause Miracles To Happen.

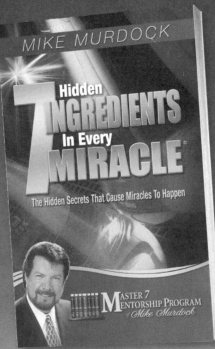

You Will Learn:

▶ How To Apply The Scriptural Formula In Every Prayer

▶ 3 Ways To Build Your Faith To Mountain-Moving Level

▶ Why Some Miracles Are Delayed Unnecessarily

▶ The Hidden Prescription For Silencir Demonic Voices In Your Environmen

The Wisdom Center

ONLY $7

B-280

Wisdom Is The Principal Thing

Add 20% For S/H

 THE WISDOM CENTER
4051 Denton Highway · Fort Worth, TX 76117

1-817-759-BOOK
1-817-759-0300

You Will Love Our Website...!
WisdomOnline.com

Miracle 7 BOOK PAK!

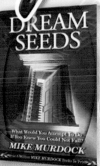

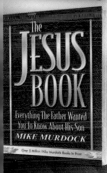

DR. MIKE MURDOCK

❶ **Dream Seeds** (Book/B-11/106pg/$12)

❷ **7 Hidden Keys to Favor** (Book/B-119/32pg/$7)

❸ **Seeds of Wisdom on Miracles** (Book/B-15/32pg/$3)

❹ **Seeds of Wisdom on Prayer** (Book/B-23/32pg/$3)

❺ **The Jesus Book** (Book/B-27/166pg/$10)

❻ **The Memory Bible on Miracles** (Book/B-208/32pg/$3)

❼ **The Mentor's Manna on Attitude** (Book/B-58/32pg/$3)

The Wisdom Center
Miracle 7 Book Pak!
Only $**30**
$54 Value
WBL-24
Wisdom Is The Principal Thing

Add 20% For S/H

MasterCard   VISA

Quantity Prices Available Upon Request

Each Wisdom Book may be purchased separately if so desired.

THE WISDOM CENTER
4051 Denton Highway • Fort Worth, TX 76117

1-817-759-BOOK
1-817-759-0300

You Will Love Our Website...!
WISDOMONLINE.COM

A

Crisis 7
BOOK PAK!

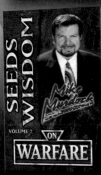

DR. MIKE MURDOCK

❶ The Survival Bible (Book/B-29/248pg/$10)

❷ Wisdom For Crisis Times (Book/B-40/112pg/$9)

❸ Seeds of Wisdom on Motivating Yourself (Book/B-171/32pg/$5)

❹ Seeds of Wisdom on Overcoming (Book/B-17/32pg/$3)

❺ Seeds of Wisdom on Warfare (Book/B-19/32pg/$3)

❻ Battle Techniques For War Weary Saints (Book/B-07/32pg/$5)

❼ Seeds of Wisdom on Adversity (Book/B-21/32pg/$3)

The Wisdom Center
**Crisis 7
Book Pak!**
Only $30 $38 Value
WBL-25
Wisdom Is The Principal Thing

Add 20% For S/H

Quantity Prices Available Upon Request

Each Wisdom Book may be purchased separately if so desired.

B

THE WISDOM CENTER
4051 Denton Highway • Fort Worth, TX 76117
1-817-759-BOOK
1-817-759-0300
You Will Love Our Website...!
WISDOMONLINE.COM

Money 7
BOOK PAK!

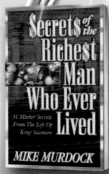
Secrets of the Richest Man Who Ever Lived
31 Master Secrets From The Life Of King Solomon
MIKE MURDOCK

The Blessing Bible
MIKE MURDOCK

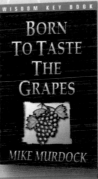
WISDOM KEY BOOK
BORN TO TASTE THE GRAPES
MIKE MURDOCK

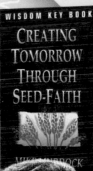
WISDOM KEY BOOK
CREATING TOMORROW THROUGH SEED-FAITH
MIKE MURDOCK

SEEDS OF WISDOM ON PROSPERITY

WISDOM KEY BOOK
SEVEN OBSTACLES TO ABUNDANT SUCCESS
MIKE MURDOCK

WISDOM KEY BOOK
TEN LIES MANY PEOPLE BELIEVE ABOUT MONEY
10 Lies
MIKE MUR...

DR. MIKE MURDOCK

❶ **Secrets of the Richest Man Who Ever Lived** (Book/B-99/179pg/$12)

❷ **The Blessing Bible** (Book/B-28/252pg/$10)

❸ **Born To Taste The Grapes** (Book/B-65/32pg/$3)

❹ **Creating Tomorrow Through Seed-Faith** (Book/B-06/32pg/$5)

❺ **Seeds of Wisdom on Prosperity** (Book/B-22/32pg/$5)

❻ **Seven Obstacles To Abundant Success** (Book/B-64/32pg/$5)

❼ **Ten Lies Many People Believe About Money** (Book/B-04/32pg/$5)

The Wisdom Center
Money 7 Book Pak!
Only $**30** $46 Value
WBL 30
Wisdom Is The Principal Thing

Add 20% For S/H

*Each Wisdom Book may be purchased separately if so desired.

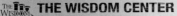

THE WISDOM CENTER
4051 Denton Highway • Fort Worth, TX 76117

1-817-759-BOOK
1-817-759-0300

You Will Love Our Website...!
WISDOMONLINE.COM

C

Career 7
Book Pak For Business People!

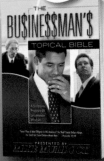
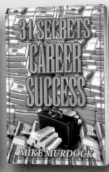

❶ The Businessman's Topical Bible (Book/B-33/384pg/$10)

❷ 31 Secrets for Career Success (Book/B-44/114pg/$10)

DR. MIKE MURDOCK

❸ 31 Scriptures Every Businessman Should Memorize (Book/B-141/32pg/$3)

❹ 7 Overlooked Keys To Effective Goal-Setting (Book/B-127/32pg/$7)

❺ 7 Rewards of Problem Solving (Book/B-118/32pg/$7)

❻ Seeds of Wisdom on Productivity (Book/B-137/32pg/$5)

❼ The Mentor's Manna on Achievement (Book/B-79/32pg/$3)

The Wisdom Center
Career 7 Book Pak!
Only $30 $45 Value
WBL-27
Wisdom Is The Principal Thing

Add 20% For S/H

Each Wisdom Book may be purchased separately if so desired.

D

THE WISDOM CENTER
4051 Denton Highway • Fort Worth, TX 76117

1-817-759-BOOK
1-817-759-0300

You Will Love Our Website...!
WISDOMONLINE.COM

101 Wisdom Keys That Have Most Changed My Life.

THE LAWS OF LIFE SERIES

The SCHOOL of WISDOM

101 WISDOM KEYS THAT HAVE MOST CHANGED MY LIFE

MIKE MURDOCK

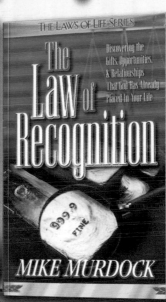

The Law of Recognition

Discovering the Gifts, Opportunities, & Relationships That God Has Already Placed In Your Life

MIKE MURDOCK

TS-42

School of Wisdom #2 Pak!

▶ What Attracts Others Toward You
▶ The Secret of Multiplying Your Financial Blessings
▶ What Stops The Flow of Your Faith
▶ Why Some Fail And Others Succeed
▶ How To Discern Your Life Assignment
▶ How To Create Currents of Favor With Others
▶ How To Defeat Loneliness
▶ 47 Keys In Recognizing The Mate God Has Approved For You
▶ 14 Facts You Should Know About Your Gifts And Talents
▶ 17 Important Facts You Should Remember About Your Weakness
▶ And Much, Much More...

The Wisdom Center
School of Wisdom #2 Pak!
Only $**30** $45 Value
PAK002
Wisdom Is The Principal Thing

Add 20% For S/H

THE WISDOM CENTER
4051 Denton Highway • Fort Worth, TX 76117
1-817-759-BOOK
1-817-759-0300

You Will Love Our Website...!
WISDOMONLINE.COM

E

The Businessman's Devotional 4 *Book Pak!*

❶ 7 Rewards of Problem Solving (Book/B-118/32pg/$7)

❷ My Personal Dream Book (Book/B-143/32pg/$5)

❸ 1 Minute Businessman's Devotional
(Book/B-42/224pg/$12)

❹ 31 Greatest Chapters In The Bible
(Book/B-54/138pg/$10)

The Wisdom Center
The Businessman's Devotional 4 Book Pak!
Only **$20** $34 Value
PAK-22
Wisdom Is The Principal Thing

Add 20% For S/H

F THE WISDOM CENTER
4051 Denton Highway • Fort Worth, TX 76117

1-817-759-BOOK
1-817-759-0300

You Will Love Our Website...!
WISDOMONLINE.COM

Millionaire-Talk

DR. MIKE MURDOCK

MY GIFT OF APPRECIATION
GIFT of Appreciation
Wisdom Is The Principal Thing

31 Things You Will Need To Become A Millionaire (2-CD's/WCPL-116)

Topics Include:

> *You Will Need Financial Heroes*
> *Your Willingness To Negotiate Everything*
> *You Must Have The Ability To Transfer Your Enthusiasm, Your Vision To Others*
> *Know Your Competition*
> *Be Willing To Train Your Team Personally As To Your Expectations*
> *Hire Professionals To Do A Professional's Job*

I have asked the Lord for 3,000 special partners who will sow an extra Seed of $58 towards our Television Outreach Ministry. Your Seed is so appreciated! Remember to request your Gift CD's, 2 Disc Volume, *31 Things You Will Need To Become A Millionaire*, when you write this week!

THE WISDOM CENTER 4051 Denton Highway • Fort Worth, TX 76117

1-817-759-BOOK
1-817-759-0300

You Will Love Our Website...!
WISDOMONLINE.COM G

The CRISIS COLLECTION

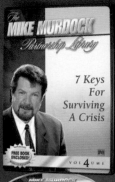

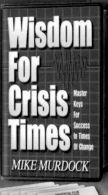

7 Keys For Surviving A Crisis

You Can Make It!

Wisdom For Crisis Times Master Keys For Success In Times Of Change
MIKE MURDOCK

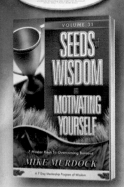

SEEDS OF WISDOM ON OVERCOMING

SEEDS OF WISDOM ON MOTIVATING YOURSELF
MIKE MURDOCK

Wisdom For Crisis Times Master Keys For Success In Times Of Change
MIKE MURDOCK

You Get All 6 For One Great Price!

❶ **7 Keys For Surviving A Crisis** (DVD/MMPL-04D/$10)

❷ **You Can Make It!** (Music CD/MMML-05/$10)

❸ **Wisdom For Crisis Times** (6 Cassettes/TS-40/$30)

❹ **Seeds of Wisdom on Overcoming** (Book/B-17/32pg/$3)

❺ **Seeds of Wisdom on Motivating Yourself** (Book/B-171/32pg/$5)

❻ **Wisdom For Crisis Times** (Book/B-40/112pg/$9)

Also Included... Two Free Bonus Books!

Each Wisdom Product may be purchased separately if so desired.

The Wisdom Center
The Crisis Collection
Only $**40** $90 Value
PAK-16
Wisdom Is The Principal Thing

Add 20% For S/H

H   **THE WISDOM CENTER** 4051 Denton Highway • Fort Worth, TX 76117

1-817-759-BOOK
1-817-759-0300

You Will Love Our Website...!
WISDOMONLINE.COM

THE TURNAROUND Collection

THE *Mike Murdock* COLLECTOR'S EDITION

WISDOM KEY BOOK

BATTLE TECHNIQUES FOR WAR WEARY SAINTS

THE WISDOM COMMENTARY 1

MIKE MURDOCK

SEEDS OF WISDOM ON OVERCOMING

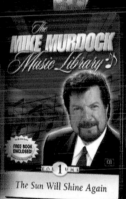

The Memory Bible on Healing

MIKE MURDOCK

WISDOM KEY BOOK

HOW TO TURN YOUR MISTAKES INTO MIRACLES

MIKE MURDOCK

The MIKE MURDOCK Partnership Library

7 Keys To Turning Your Life Around

FREE BOOK ENCLOSED!

VOL 3 UME

DVD

The MIKE MURDOCK Music Library

FREE BOOK ENCLOSED!

VOLUME 1
The Sun Will Shine Again

❶ The Wisdom Commentary Vol. 1 (Book/B-136/256pg/52 Topics/$25)

❷ Battle Techniques For War Weary Saints (Book/B-07/32pg/$5)

❸ Seeds of Wisdom on Overcoming (Book/B-17/32pg/$3)

❹ The Memory Bible on Healing (Book/B-196/32pg/$5)

❺ How To Turn Your Mistakes Into Miracles (Book/B-56/32pg/$5)

❻ 7 Keys To Turning Your Life Around (DVD/MMPL-03D/$10)

❼ The Sun Will Shine Again (Music CD/MMML-01/$10)

The Wisdom Center
The Turnaround Collection
Only $40
$63 Value
PAK-15
Wisdom Is The Principal Thing

Add 20% For S/H

*Each Wisdom Product may be purchased separately if so desired.

THE WISDOM CENTER
4051 Denton Highway • Fort Worth, TX 76117

1-817-759-BOOK
1-817-759-0300

You Will Love Our Website...!
WISDOMONLINE.COM

Favor 4!

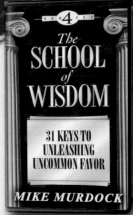

This Collection of Wisdom Will Change The Seasons of Your Life Forever!

1 The School of Wisdom #4 / 31 Keys To Unleashing Uncommon Favor...Tape Series (6 Cassettes/TS-44/$30)

2 The Hidden Power of Right Words... Master 7 Mentorship Program of Mike Murdock (CD/WCPL-27/$10)

3 7 Hidden Keys to Favor (Book/B-119/32pg/$7)

4 Seeds of Wisdom on Obedience (Book/B-20/32pg/$5)

The Wisdom Center
Favor 4 Collection!
Only **$35** $52 Value
PAK-12
Wisdom Is The Principal Thing

Add 20% For S/H

Each Wisdom Product may be purchased separately if so desired.

J **THE WISDOM CENTER** 4051 Denton Highway • Fort Worth, TX 76117
1-817-759-BOOK
1-817-759-0300

You Will Love Our Website...!
WISDOMONLINE.COM

Financial $ecrets.

31 REASONS PEOPLE DO NOT RECEIVE THEIR FINANCIAL HARVEST

THE 31 DAY MENTORSHIP PROGRAM

MIKE MURDOCK

VI-17

Buy One... Receive The Second One FREE!

The Wisdom Center · Wisdom Is The Principal Thing

VIDEO

7 KEYS to 1000 TIMES MORE

The Lord God Of Your Fathers Make You A Thousand Times So Many More As You Are, And Bless You, As He Hath Promised You! Deuteronomy 1:11

MIKE MURDOCK

VI-16

Your Financial World Will Change Forever.

Video 2-Pak!

➤ 8 Scriptural Reasons You Should Pursue Financial Prosperity

➤ The Secret Prayer Key You Need When Making A Financial Request To God

➤ The Weapon of Expectation And The 5 Miracles It Unlocks

➤ How To Discern Those Who Qualify To Receive Your Financial Assistance

➤ How To Predict The Miracle Moment God Will Schedule Your Financial Breakthrough

➤ Habits of Uncommon Achievers

➤ The Greatest Success Law I Ever Discovered

➤ How To Discern Your Place of Assignment, The Only Place Financial Provision Is Guaranteed

➤ 3 Secret Keys In Solving Problems For Others

The Wisdom Center
Video 2-Pak!
Only **$30** $60 Value
VIPAK-01
Wisdom Is The Principal Thing

Add 20% For S/H

*Each Wisdom Product may be purchased separately if so desired.

THE WISDOM CENTER 4051 Denton Highway • Fort Worth, TX 76117
1-817-759-BOOK
1-817-759-0300

You Will Love Our Website...!
WISDOMONLINE.COM

K

THE WISDOM BIBLE

Partnership Edition

Over 120 Wisdom Study Guides Included Such As:

- *10 Qualities of Uncommon Achievers*
- *18 Facts You Should Know About The Anointing*
- *21 Facts To Help You Identify Those Assigned To You*
- *31 Facts You Should Know About Your Assignment*
- *8 Keys That Unlock Victory In Every Attack*
- *22 Defense Techniques To Remember During Seasons of Personal Attack*
- *20 Wisdom Keys And Techniques To Remember During An Uncommon Battle*
- *11 Benefits You Can Expect From God*
- *31 Facts You Should Know About Favor*
- *The Covenant of 58 Blessings*
- *7 Keys To Receiving Your Miracle*
- *16 Facts You Should Remember About Contentious People*
- *5 Facts Solomon Taught About Contracts*
- *7 Facts You Should Know About Conflict*
- *6 Steps That Can Unlock Your Self-Confidence*
- *And Much More!*

Your Partnership makes such a difference in The Wisdom Center Outreach Ministries. I wanted to place a Gift in your hand that could last a lifetime for you and your family...**The Wisdom Study Bible.**

40 Years of Personal Notes...this Partnership Edition Bible contains 160 pages of my Personal Study Notes...that could forever change your Bible Study of The Word of God. This **Partnership Edition...**is my personal **Gift of Appreciation** when you sow your Sponsorship Seed of $1,000 to help us complete The Prayer Center and TV Studio Complex. An Uncommon Seed Always Creates An Uncommon Harvest!

Mike

Thank you from my heart for your Seed of Obedience (Luke 6:38).

L

THE WISDOM CENTER 4051 Denton Highway • Fort Worth, TX 76117

1-817-759-BOOK
1-817-759-0300

You Will Love Our Website...!
WISDOMONLINE.COM

This Gift of Appreciation Will Change Your Bible Study For The Rest of Your Life.

The *Wisdom Bible*

MY GIFT OF APPRECIATION
Celebrating
Your Sponsorship Seed
of $1,000 For The
Prayer Center & TV
Studio Complex
Wisdom Is The Principal Thing
B-235

THE WISDOM CENTER   1-817-759-BOOK
4051 Denton Highway • Fort Worth, TX 76117   1-817-759-0300

You Will Love Our Website...!
WISDOMONLINE.COM   M

Spirit Music

TS-59

LOVE SONGS TO THE HOLY SPIRIT
Written In The Secret Place

THE HOLY SPIRIT HANDBOOK
What You Need To Know About Your
Daily Companion, The Holy Spirit
Volume 1
MIKE MURDOCK

The Wisdom Center
Free Book
ENCLOSED!
B-100 ($15 Value)
Wisdom Is The Principal Thing

Songs...

1. A Holy Place
2. Anything You Want
3. Everything Comes From You
4. Fill This Place With Your Presence
5. First Thing Every Morning
6. Holy Spirit, I Want To Hear You
7. Holy Spirit, Move Again
8. Holy Spirit, You Are Enough
9. I Don't Know What I Would Do Without You
10. I Let Go (of Anything That Stops Me)
11. I'll Just Fall On You
12. I Love You, Holy Spirit
13. I'm Building My Life Around You
14. I'm Giving Myself To You
15. I'm In Love! I'm In Love!
16. I Need Water (Holy Spirit, You're My Well)
17. In The Secret Place
18. In Your Presence, I'm Always Changed

19. In Your Presence (Miracles Are Born)
20. I've Got To Live In Your Presence
21. I Want To Hear Your Voice
22. I Will Do Things Your Way
23. Just One Day At A Time
24. Meet Me In The Secret Place
25. More Than Ever Before
26. Nobody Else Does What You Do
27. No No Walls!
28. Nothing Else Matters Anymore (Since I've Been In The Presence of You Lord)
29. Nowhere Else
30. Once Again You've Answered
31. Only A Fool Would Try (To Live Without You)
32. Take Me Now
33. Teach Me How To Please You
34. There's No Place I'd Rather Be
35. Thy Word Is All That Matters

36. When I Get In Your Presence
37. You're The Best Thing (That's E Happened To Me)
38. You Are Wonderful
39. You've Done It Once
40. You Keep Changing Me
41. You Satisfy

The Wisdom Center
6 Tapes / Only $30 *
PAK007
Wisdom Is The Principal Thing

Add 20% For S/H

N   THE WISDOM CENTER
4051 Denton Highway • Fort Worth, TX 76117
1-817-759-BOOK
1-817-759-0300
You Will Love Our Website...!
WISDOMONLINE.COM

YOUR ASSIGNMENT IS YOUR DISTINCTION FROM OTHERS.

THE ASSIGNMENT:
THE DREAM & THE DESTINY
MIKE MURDOCK

THE ASSIGNMENT:
THE ANOINTING & THE ADVERSITY
MURDOCK

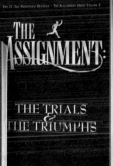
THE ASSIGNMENT:
THE TRIALS & THE TRIUMPHS
MIKE MURDOCK

THE ASSIGNMENT:
THE PAIN & THE PASSION
MIKE MURDOCK

Assignment 4 Book Pak!

Uncommon Wisdom For Discovering Your Life Assignment.

❶ The Dream & The Destiny
Vol 1 (Book/B-74/164 pg/$12)

❷ The Anointing & The Adversity
Vol 2 (Book/B-75/192 pg/$12)

❸ The Trials & The Triumphs
Vol 3 (Book/B-97/160 pg/$12)

❹ The Pain & The Passion
Vol 4 (Book/B-98/144 pg/$12)

*Each Wisdom Book may be purchased separately if so desired.

The Wisdom Center
Assignment 4 Book Pak!
Only $30 $48 Value
WBL 14
Wisdom Is The Principal Thing

Add 20% For S/H04

THE WISDOM CENTER
4051 Denton Highway • Fort Worth, TX 76117

1-817-759-BOOK
1-817-759-0300

You Will Love Our Website...!
WISDOMONLINE.COM

O

JOIN THE Wisdom Key 3000 TODAY!

Thank You For Joining The Wisdom Key 3000!

Pursuing...Proclaiming And Publishing The Wisdom Of God

Will You Become My Ministry Partner In The Work of God?

Dear Friend,

God has connected us!

I have asked The Holy Spirit for 3000 Special Partners who will plant a monthly Seed of $58.00 to help me bring the gospel around the world. (58 represents 58 kinds of blessings in the Bible.)

Will you become my monthly Faith Partner in The Wisdom Key 3000? Your monthly Seed of $58.00 is so powerful in helping heal broken lives. When you sow into the work of God, 4 Miracle Harvests are guaranteed in Scripture, Isaiah 58...

- ▶ Uncommon <u>Health</u> (Isaiah 58)
- ▶ Uncommon <u>Wisdom</u> For <u>Decision-Making</u> (Isaiah 58)
- ▶ Uncommon <u>Financial Favor</u> (Isaiah 58)
- ▶ Uncommon <u>Family Restoration</u> (Isaiah 58)

Your Faith Partner,

Mike Murdock

P.S. Please clip the coupon attached and return it to me today, so I can rush the Wisdom Key Partnership Pak to you...or call me at 1-817-759-0300.

THE Covenant OF Fifty-Eight Blessings

101 WISDOM KEYS

The Blessing BIBLE

THE CRAZIEST instruction GOD EVER GAVE ME
The Personal Testimony That Has Unlocked Miracles For Millions

MIKE MURDOCK

WISDOM KEY 3000 PARTNERSHIP SEED BOOK

A Very Personal Word From Mike Murdock

PP-03

☐ **Yes Mike, I want to join The Wisdom Key 3000.**
   Please rush The Wisdom Key Partnership Pak to me today!

☐ **Enclosed is my first monthly Seed-Faith Promise of:**
   ☐ **$58** ☐ **Other $_____.**

☐ CHECK   ☐ MONEY ORDER   ☐ AMEX   ☐ DISCOVER   ☐ MASTERCARD   ☐ VISA

Credit Card # _____   Exp. ____/___

Signature _____

Name _____ Birth Date ____/___

Address _____

City _____ State _____ Zip _____

Phone _____ E-Mail _____

Your Seed-Faith Offerings are used to support The Wisdom Center, and all of its programs. The Wisdom Center reserves the right to redirect funds as needed in order to carry out our charitable purpose. In the event The Wisdom Center receives more funds for the project than needed, the excess will be used for another worthy outreach. (Your transactions may be electronically deposited.)

WK-30-

P THE WISDOM CENTER
4051 Denton Highway • Fort Worth, TX 76117

1-817-759-**BOOK**
1-817-759-0300

You Will Love Our Website...!
WISDOMONLINE.COM